Disciples
of an
Uncertain Season
and
Other Poems

Larry Holland

Logan House Press
Books Are Heavy

Disciples of an Uncertain Season and Other Poems

Scott McIntosh, Editor

ISBN: 0-9674123-3-1 $12.00

Logan House Press
Route 1 Box 154
Winside, Nebraska 68790

email to:
loganhousepress@alltell.net

Printed in the United States of America by
Morris Publishing • 3212 E Hwy 30
Kearney, Nebraska 68847

Acknowledgements

These poems first appeared in the following magazines and anthologies:

Calapooya Collage—"All the Way," "Maggie," "Spring Follows Old Flyways," "Home School," and "This is My Body."

Hurakan—"Eleven Days."

Kansas Quarterly—"Sand" (reprinted in *Poetry of Nebraska*) and "Walk on Water."

Nebraska English Journal—"Reward" and "How to Acquire a Beard."

Nebraska Territory—"Turtle Stew," "This First Cold Morning of Fall," "A Beautiful Valley This," "Shooting," "Niobrara River Crossing," "The Length of Shadows," and "Blood Brothers" (1990 Elkhorn Poetry Prize winner, reprinted in *Logan House Anthology of 21st Century American Poetry*).

Plainsongs—"Scot Magic" (under another title) and "Friday Night."

Platte Valley Review—"Destiny."

Tenth Street Miscellany—"Wrong Foot Forward."

The Nebraska Review—"Among Cedars," "The Eye Altering Alters All," "Out of Season," "Smokeshack Payoff," "Of Patriarchs, Dowagers, Cats and Zucchini," and "An Act of God."

West Branch—"The Whisper of Bones Grating" (reprinted in *The Decade Dance*) and "Mid-January Thaw."

Wind Literary Journal—"West of Omaha, by Way of New Caledonia" and "Mutability."

Yarrow—"Could You Have Blinked and Not Seen It and Been Saved?" (reprinted in *Out of Season: An Anthology of Work By and About Young People Who Died*) and "Vagrants" (reprinted in *Logan House Anthology of 21st Century American Poetry*). Both poems reprinted in *As Far as I Can See: Contemporary Writers of the Mid-Plains.*

Editor's Note

At the time of Larry Holland's death in March of 1999, *Disciples of an Uncertain Season*, published just the fall before, had virtually sold out. This volume reprints *Disciples* in its entirety with the addition of a number of poems previously available only in magazines and journals. An introduction and an afterword by his friends and fellow poets Red Shuttleworth and Neil Harrison have been added as well. This enterprise has been a labor of love, and this collection is dedicated to the friends, family and students of Larry Holland.

—The Editor
July 2001

Introduction

"There weren't another other way to be."
                                  —Billy Joe Shaver

Larry Holland threw a party shortly after I met him. He and his wife, Becky, were in a duplex apartment in Norfolk at the time, one of those places relatively easy to keep clean when both folks are working. I went to have a few drinks and get to know new colleagues at Northeast Community College back in early 1983. Larry and Becky were gracious and dressed in their most comfortable dress-for-success duds. Their friends were tricked-out in similar middle-of-the-road, non-offensive garments. It looked like a convention of third grade teachers and everyone knows, or ought to know, there ain't nothin' dumber or more boring than third grade teachers and their shopkeeper in-laws. I had a whiskey—quickly—and hauled ass out of there.

The strange part was that Lar was playing Waylon Jennings' record, *Honky Tonk Heroes*, which celebrates desperation, bruised love, and the consequences of the Gonzo Way (you might say, if you were formally educated at some mid-level state college, Existential). I don't think anybody there was gettin' the message from ol' Waylon as he worked Billy Joe Shaver's writing over a stuttering guitar.

A few days later, Lar asked, "Why'd you leave so soon?" People in ruts, the self-defeating ones, usually don't admit it or know it or want to discuss ruts.

"All your friends are dead," I said.

To his credit, I suppose, Lar never abandoned his life-like pals, but he did add real life (new books, new friends, horses, cattle, and writing) to his remaining time. He did that most improbable thing: he truly created himself anew. He became, first, a poet and an editor of a literary journal, *Elkhorn Review*. Maybe he enlivened some of his old, life-like friends with poems on hunting, horses, taking a drink with a worthy friend, and hiking in rough country with his grand pal, Neil Harrison. What is for certain is that the poems are good and deserve to be read for the avid-hearted life within them, for the wisdom that comes out of hard-earned change, and for the joy found in the physical life.

Lar's editing work at *Elkhorn Review*, his creation of the Nebraska Literary Festival (a lot of academic dick-sucks are trying to steal that claim to creation), and his running of the summer Elkhorn Writers' Conference stole the literary thunder from Omaha and Lincoln. For a few short ticks of the clock (1984-1988), folks had to go to Norfolk to participate in the lasting, primary making of vital plains writing (deep, deep apologies to Jim Brummels here, for his Plains Writers Series pre-dates Lar's efforts and was the partnering beast over in Wayne).

Along with Barbara Schmitz, I shared Lar's vision and labor on the *Elkhorn Review* and related projects. But make no mistake, Lar increasingly became proprietary and we should always acknowledge that he was the principle go-to-guy when we needed to get something done at Northeast Community College, which paid for the whole deal (as more colleges should to keep their promise to be their regions' cultural prods and repositories).

I'm proud to say Lar was my friend. I drank with him, argued poetry with him, and shared in the dreaming of what we could do for poetry. On more than a few go-rounds, Lar saved me from a quick firing. I used to, routinely, go over to what Lar tagged "Bumbledick Hall" (administration building) to tell one or another paper-shuffling, butt-pick dean that suicide was the only honorable way out of that life. Lar was essentially our English Chairman, so the offended dean, none of 'em manly at all, would phone Lar to whine. First, Lar would say to me, "Why do you do things like that? I've known so-and-so for twenty years and he ain't all bad. You gotta stop, Red." Then he'd go over to visit with the wounded dean and, from what I later learned, he'd say, "Red's right. You do-nothing people should eat the working end of a handgun." The great thing was that when Lar chewed their butts, they felt guilty and, sooner or later, the literary adventure would benefit.

Before too long, Lar and Becky moved into a huge, comfortable house in Norfolk (though Lar would episodically consider buying a house and ground near Winside). The big house had once been owned by country singer/songwriter Jim Casey and it was a good place to get drunk and talk poetry. Upstairs was their guest room for visiting poets, a darned magical place to bunk. The walls were covered with photos of Bill Kloefkorn, Paul Zarzyski, and a host of other poets who matter.

Lar would show up at our place in Winside a lot. He kept his horses at Jim Brummels' ranch a mile away, so we were a convenient hangout. Lar'd find a safe spot for his wide-brimmed, high-crowned Resistol, light his pipe, pop open a beer, and get going on his latest poetry enthusiasm or he'd vent about the do-nothings-for-poetry at the University of Nebraska-Lincoln or he'd talk about his cowboy dreams, and we always hated to see him go outside and start-up his old green Ford pick-up and we'd try to get him to stay for supper.

Goddamnit, Lar's gone now, and hardly a day goes by that I don't miss him. He was a great letter-writer, so we stayed close after I cut a trail from Nebraska to Nevada in 1988, and we'd talk some on the phone. He'd come into his own and we expected grand poems for years to come. Now we must treasure what we do have, these fine poems by Larry Holland, who wasn't afraid to change for the better: horse 'n' cow poet, poet of friendship, poet of love and uncooked life.

Sometimes Lar rode reckless and worked his horse too hard, but he had learned to go full-tilt, finally, to take chances when others might cut 'n' run or just stay home with a rented video rated PG and a bowl of popcorn, to take the sort of chances that create poems that must be read and read again to find out there really ain't another other way to be.

—Red Shuttleworth
Sawtooth Saloon
Arco, Idaho
June 21, 2001

Contents

Disciples

of an

Uncertain

Season

For the Grandfathers,
who have shadowed this track.

Thanks

Any writer owes a great debt of gratitude to a number of people. I wish to acknowledge here such debt to the following:

—to Becky, whose fine eyes had first look at most of these poems;

—to Les Whipp, who invited me to the Nebraska Writing Project, which gave a jumpstart to my notion of writing;

—to Don Welch, with whom I've exchanged more Platte Valley lore than either of us knew we knew;

—to Harry Humes, who had the nerve to publish several pieces early, and became a good friend and trusted critic;

—to JV Brummels, who has pushed my writing, one way or another, for several years;

—to Hairsn (Neil Harrison), with whom I've ridden and canoed many trails and rivers, and who has provided a wealth of material;

and most of all

—to Linda Hasselstrom, Paul "Whisky" Zarzyski and Red Shuttleworth, whose boundless faith in my writing, determination that I do something with it, and unfailing friendship forced them to offer the sharp criticism and occasional swift kick that gave me the notion much of this material was worth fussing over.

Muchas gracias, amigos.

Foreword

Years ago, while on surveillance with a friend who was also trying to stay on the tail of a Russian agent who had surreptitiously entered this country, we talked of where we had grown up, he in Chicago and I in the small towns of Nebraska. At one point he said that when he retired as an architect and millionaire (he has become both), he would like to move to Nebraska where he could live on a ranch of a few acres. Wouldn't take much, he said, to get him started—a steer and couple of cows. It was night when he told me this, and I remember smiling a fox-tail smile in the city's dark.

Larry Holland would give a good buckskin snort to my friend's ignorance, then write a story in which a fellow from Chicago, coming to the Sandhills of Nebraska, introduces a steer to his heifers. The sun would be hot, the wind kicking up from the south, the man stylishly leaning on a rough-cut fence in his L.L. Bean western wear, wondering why his steer wouldn't steer. He would stand there a long time, the particles of his learning, like a dust devil, circling the ignorance of a hollow.

There is no hollow to Larry Holland's best poems. There is only that core which comes from growing up in a place and digging into it. Seamus Heaney, the great Irish poet of our times, said that his father dug with a peat-spade, but that he, the son, would dig with his pen. There is a similar temperament and resolution in Larry Holland's life and verse. His words smack of hands-on, leathered work. He is dead-on when he looks, putting a bead to the center of his sight. And he knows how to make his spirit sweat. His grasslands, to paraphrase Robert Frost, are the right place for hard-working love; he doesn't know where it's likely to go better.

Nature poets abound. Some of them attempt to put imaginative geographies on real landscapes, and their dislocations are quickly, and regrettably, exposed. Others are travelers, knowing just enough about a place to write a faddish verse about it. Because their stakes are low and their glimpses passing, their verse is tourist trap stuff at its worst. The best poets of place can make both a place and its inhabitants transcendent. Initially luminous, their poems brand our memories with felt thoughts. And only the very best of these keep going, moving away from their localities, keeping their heads up in strange lands among strange peoples, but never forgetting who or what parented them. Wherever they go, they walk as certain disciples in very certain seasons.

After you have read the poems in this book go back to "Out of Season" and "Could You Have Blinked and Not Seen It and Been Saved?". Give those two poems another chance to work on the hairs on the back of your neck. Then look at the skill that has gone into their writing; like his mother, Larry Holland is careful not to bruise the things he feeds us. Especially death and grief. Note, too, the way he exercises great care in writing his phrases and lines (there is no unwellmade verse still fashionable in our sloppy times). And consider further the maturity he demonstrates in letting the revelations of these poems come to trim, which is reminiscent of waiting patiently for a trophy buck in a tree-stand. His stakes are high. What he asks of these poems are no penny ante raises or nickel pots.

We need skill to know if we have done something well. Larry Holland has that kind of skill, and so much more. To use his own words, he possesses the talent to make a poem's pulse thump against the silence of its own making. Like the land he loves, he has come to own a poem's terrain as much as it owns him, and at his best, his riding out is always riding in.

—Don Welch
Kearney, Nebraska
1998

"Dark is a Way and Light is a Place"
—Dylan Thomas

She squinted at the Sunday crossword puzzle,
too excited or too short or both to sit.
From a world of boxes nearly filled
she came back. "What kinds of poems
will you read to those people?"
Her pencil, gentle, uncovered a word,
an archeologist spooning dust from bones.
About a black man dead under a boxcar wheel,
I told her, hoboes, food and drink, and one of
innocence lost when a son's going
left guilt he couldn't take with him.

Grey eyes past eighty-five
years of their own perception
pored the last row of empty spaces.
"Where do you find the words?"
They're inside, I told her, wanting out.
"Like times you know you'll never get back?"

Softly as a woman with a new baby might, she smiled
and filled, just as certain of life, the last blank.
"Just like that," we said together and stared,
the words staring back, blind eyes
daring us to let them lead us
into the catacombs of memory.

> *for Mom*

Disciples of an Uncertain Season

Destiny

A dry fly cast
through a smoke of real mosquitoes
pinpoints the rush of a trout
scouring the bottomside of a mirror
to break glass and suck in
knotted hair for its gut,
steel for the lip.

for Bill Fursteneau

Whether We Know or Not

When you said, "It's coming ice,
I'm not up to going that far
to check. Besides, God knows,
whether we know or not,
they're cranes, or not,"
I looked even harder
for the red eye-patch
and how they would move
slowly, proud thin ghosts
on legs like jointed sticks.
"They don't look right,
may be Canadas."
The possible first of the great birds
whose thousands sing spring north,
a dozen scattered tall in winter mist.

Ears strained against the wind
for the seductive lilt
heard only sleet ricochet off coats.
Past my whitened sleeve
you looked into a grey deeper
than I knew, listened
to what I couldn't hear, a message
brought by long-throated disciples
of an uncertain season.

Spring Follows Old Flyways

Across a moonless night
early spring clouds
bounce odd reflections off city lights.
Gaggles of Hutchinsons and Snows
cackle in circles, sort directions
from a fog of genetics and false landmarks.
Agonizing her mother's flight
through twelve senile years
shrouded in a nursing home,
Mom was thrown off course
by the same cruel design.
She found, in nine fewer years,
her own last pattern.

Now late May combiners
string south out of Canada like gypsies
drawn to pockets of sunbelt wheatfields.
I'm pointed north
thinking how everything moves
on seasoned wingbeats
toward the same hopeful end,
how three months from now
hard red wheat will make Montana shovels ring
and geese near the Arctic Circle
still weeks from the cold
will pack their breasts with instinct,
ache to push their long V's south.

The First Cold Morning of Fall

Cattle are skittish as crows
scouting a weather front,
sometimes blow with a storm until
a herd of eyes and noses drifts shut.
Steered by wing and tail pinions,
a crow foraging roadbed or field
knows salvation comes
on the first cold wind.

Does it matter what a crow knows?
Does its brain, perhaps a matter smaller,
greyer to better match its feathers,
have all my folds and synapses?
I can layer silk, cotton, canvas,
pull a wide brim down
over a squint tightened against
the wind's bite. Are its thoughts
complex as a steer's, head held low
to morning bales, brown eyes glowing
vague as sundogs under black curly brow,
slobber blown in spiderwebs
from lips anxious, as if this hay
may be the last before the final blow?
Other than a pickup horn that stirs
a murder of crows operating on roadkill radar
into a marvel of sideslips and wingbeats,
a crow knows no bounds.

———•———

Sand

Old Tom lived
north of Meadow Grove.

North five miles
up to the ridge
that is the sand
backbone of Yellow Banks
you see first
from the section corner
green against blue-black sky
two cottonwoods
stark above the sand
ruts that mark the way
to the weathered barn.

Tom started that barn
to mark the fall
his first son was born.
He planted those trees
the spring the second
boy was born.

The second boy
went five miles
south to the river
his seven-year-old play
didn't have the strength
to fight his way out of.
The first son
survived (too long,
some said) everything
but the draft
that sent him
east to the jungle
he couldn't find
his way out of.

From the cottonwoods,
barkless white
in the afternoon,
you see the barn's lean,
imperceptible almost,
like an old man
who's seen too long.

Mid-January Thaw

"Doc says my lungs are like leather."
Dad hadn't put a word to what coal miners
call Black Lung, but I guessed sixty years
working lumber into sawdust and cabinets
made *emphysema* sound about right. And when
he'd say ten steps in the cold would take
all the air he had, I knew lives shaped in dust
choke on the same gamble.

This time of year, warm days pushed by
evening skies the color of good lungs,
sundown comes fast and cold
drifts deep and sudden around sockfeet
propped up by the unlit fireplace. Now
dark goes down hard as the first pull
off a just-opened bottle. Such days
are a run false as a short streak
at a Vegas crap table, just enough
to make a greenhorn watching the rake
build his pile of chips,
blow for luck on fresh dice and
imagine easy street near as
one more fistful of dream.

Soon, when the Arctic fronts come
and come again, the right word
won't matter. New snow
will cover old tracks until
the air carries the sound of blue ice
cracking and heartache is the feel
that even April could come up snake eyes.

Smokeshack Payoff—Cal-Ida Lumber Company, Auburn, CA, 1957

The foreman handed pay envelopes
round at morning break. Noon
whistle sounds. Like water
drawn to a siphon they hobnail
from corners of the mill down the hill
swinging lunch boxes, the promise
of paid bills a whirlpool
at the smokeshack door.
The tide of bi-monthly ritual tips a bench—
this noon there'll be no sitting or eating—
men will kneel again to breathe
life on dice that bank off wood.
Fresh cash cheers sweating fists, as wives
waiting for dinner might wring hands anxious in aprons
for scrapes of boots on porches,
children with innocent leers
ready to pounce on a lunch box
the moment the door is closed.

for Pete Pascuzzi, Carl-Louis Pritchard,
Moreno Bertelozzi, Donovan Holland,
the Trianos brothers and Moose

Out of Season

This morning like a blast
from the gun in your own hand
the news of your undoing scudded over us,
so much cumulus bucking a northeast wind
and lightning charging again our nerves
with the smell of mortality.

No matter that it was fall work,
this afternoon our frustration cleared
iris and peonies past their season
and trumpet vine reaching a sprawled tangle
into cracks in the foundation of the house.
We cut and pulled bulbs and roots
that surrendered dust easy
as leaves scatter on a dry wind.

Late this evening
the drooping yellow eye
of the waning moon hung
to blink shut in rising thunderheads.
On this hot and muggy night,
are the spots on this paper
raindrops, tears or sweat?

Two days from now
the weathered shell of a mother will follow
a hearse real as her worst dream
to a plot of prairie dug to seven feet
beside a mound waiting to be thrown and tamped
on hopes seeded with the shadow of memories.
Now the stuffed black trash bag
sags heavy, a wet plastic orb shining
in a dark and rain-slick alley.

for Steve

———•◄—

Could You Have Blinked
and Not Seen It and Been Saved?

Seven years old I stared unblinking
at a black barrel leaned
against the wall you slumped against
after death's blank stare
had pulled you past gravity.
Days later, still as your blood
pooled black on the floor,
I saw you again,
the black dot in the corner of your right eye
proof you wouldn't wake from this sleep.
Forty years beyond your coffin
you and I remain motionless forever
in a black hole of the mind,
two photographs
that swallowed our innocence.

Children of other ages do it again and
again, go in wars and crashes,
take themselves in numbers
those left try to understand,
to understand that
action simple and almost
motionless as a forefinger
curled around time's trigger
frames life surely
as a shot in an album.

for Bob

Shooting

On the range
you'll need a pair of .38 hulls
stuck open-end into your ears—
big-bore muzzle-bark will set
anvils and hammers in your head ringing
louder than real ones in blacksmith shops.
You'll want a glove to handle
matched fiddleback maple grips
when the shock of 240 grains of lead
forces a big frame into your palm,
G's you'll feel all the way
to your shoulder. That's on the range
where round after round of concentration
conditions eyes and finger to pull
down on the real thing.

On stand
you'll need to feel movement,
a shadow, off to the side, still
in the brush—flick of ear, glint
of light off antler tine, leaf-whisper
touched by one double-teardrop hoof.

Now you'll want to thumb
back the hammer slow, forefinger
holding back the trigger
so a cylinder packed with hollow points
will skip one click and muffle two more.
That's when movement imperceptible
as hair raising on the back of the neck
takes full shape. Wait until the buck comes
broadside, head down, then extend the arms,
off hand cradling grip hand, the two
a picture of supplication, sights lined
where you know vertebrae will shift
smooth on cartilage-cushion to
turn his head away. That's the time
a finger's polished squeeze
will answer the brain's slight impulse.

You won't hear or feel
the jolt of a gun's jump
blot out the buck's last lunge.
You may hear, as if from a dark distance
and for the first time, your own pulse thump
against a silence of your own making.

Among Cedars

Front legs working like a Tennessee Walker,
the doe, tail tucked to cover the white rump,
precise as dry leaves turned to powder crosses
five yards from the stand. Dark red flecks
lightly wet a hoof-turned leaf. The sun
settles into the top of the thicket, rising
shadows turn tree trunks grey. Robins, juncos,
downy woodpeckers among the cedars play
their day's last chorus. Three squirrels
scratch among the leaves, their last search
before dark a grating sound like caution
rubbed on the edge of disaster.
A horned owl megaphones its question against
the lone cottonwood spire, against the red sky
stark as an arrow through the lungs.
Night fills the recesses where roots meet leaves
and turn to bark, drifts shut the day like black snow.

"The Eye Altering Alters All"
—William Blake, *The Mental Traveler*

Each black hoof is
two precise teardrops in the snow,
the white outline of the muzzle
down and up as if fighting gravity;
brown eyes pin my eyes open,
no muscles move, no hair ripples.

Each time her head turns,
the rifle, obsessed by movement,
comes down by quarter-inches,
like clicks of a scope—she stops,
it stops; she moves, it settles
its eye on her ribcage and leads
her fast walk nearly across the clearing.

She jumps and is back in the brush,
pink flecks on the snow confirmation
of her churned breath, lungs useless
before she hears the blast. Eight jumps
I do not see slide her against the base
of an ash. Dusk settles the sound
of fog and two inches of new snow
among the cottonwoods.

Niobrara River Crossing

Late summer and flies. Shoulders
the grey of early-season mule deer
quiver beside me in Nebraska's Sandhills
south of Merriman under river-sifted bluffs
where the four-point forded last fall.
The Arab—doe-eyed, nostrils flared, ears
like spearheads ready for the Infidel—
seems almost ambivalent, caught
perhaps in near-recollection of desert
in this land of grassy dunes.
Somewhere east, downriver,
a locust's drying wing-chirr
hangs like a season ending.

To add familiar sound
I tell the horse
the buck crossed north, head low,
to does in the cedars.
Each hoof delicate as matched teardrops
cleared knee-deep water, each down again
between limestone ridges.
Later, I say, I would wade
to find him curled as if asleep
beneath hanging cedar boughs,
the only sound sand-muffled water.

This time, I say, I stay dry.
Keep your head low to see the ridges,
put each lucky shoe in the right place,
take us across that sand and rock bottom.
There's grass on the other side,
grass your ancestors didn't even dream.
I'll loosen your cinch there,
lean back against a sand bank,
listen to the locust's prophecy,
conjure pipe smoke into
this fall's grass-country venison.

for Richard Cobb

—————•⊷—————

Reward

What we knew was
we were on Tom Horn's land. Not
Tom Horn, bounty hunter, hanged
one day after jury deliberation decided
he'd shot a boy off a rail fence
at two hundred thirteen yards
with a .45-60 Creedmore-sighted Winchester.
This was the other Tom Horn,
uncle of your daughter's husband.

It was near Buzzard's Roost,
Custer County canyon country
wild as the stories that had the James boys
ride that way more than once. Oldtimers
swore they'd seen the Daltons, and that
the Ketchums had a hideout there before
Print Olive put his brand on their hides.
We talked about them all that day and knew
little more than two generations removed might.
The three-point came early
out of the plum brush
into a shot he'd never hear,
the two-point some later—you'd seen him
go into a small draw a mile south.

In the snapshot
your three-year-old granddaughter
and her small friend, clear-eyed as dawn,
admire wild and fading beauty.
Those two bucks hang over them
from a branch of the old elm
behind your grey-block garage,
antler-up, like a scene
in a Maine hunting camp.
Supper was a picture we didn't take,
but that night we ate liver and onions
like we were facing the gallows.

We've not been back.
It wasn't Maine whitetail woods. It was
four sections of the best native grass on the Plains.
Mule deer still run the old outlaw trails. Disease
years ago brought down the elm.
Your Winchester's been racked,
quiet as a buck in the brushy draws of memory.
Now your granddaughter and her husband
will fix venison liver with onions of a fall,
certain as bounty hunters headed for the bank,
reward chits in their pockets.

for Jo and Dan

Tracks At the Edge of the Night

I face due east in the pre-dawn.
Last night's track snakes under my stand
in sixteen inches of new snow.
Deer in this dark will be a long time coming.

Dawn comes sharp and high, dark stays
on the trail. Thirty yards from light
movement of dark on dark calls
time. Perceptible as a blink
stillness stands in the shape of a whitetail,
the sun through the trees outlining back hair
ruffed against early winter, puffs of fog rising
off the black dot of a nose.

The squeeze of the trigger
splatters white dawn blood-red.
The buck bolts twenty yards, its head
a wall mount backed by ash,
antlers and brambles a final tangle.

Blood
Brothers

Turtle Stew: Beauty in the Pot of the Beholder

She said, "I had a nightmare last night,
you and your partner cooking
a turtle in our kitchen
for Friday supper."
"You must have dozed off just before
I said you are invited."

He'd got his first with a meathook—
"Not a hayhook, just this old meathook,
Don't know why it was in my car"—
hooked it under the chin out of the marsh-
slime hard by the road. One he whacked
with an ax through its alligator-back,
others he'd arrowed, speared and caught
on baited hooks. But the easiest
appeared in a five-gallon bucket
left at the office, prehistoric, reptilian,
like a wife's troubled sleep
clawing at the edge of the unconscious.

Built around hunger mistaken for cussedness,
lifespan enough to reach sea-turtle size
and a taste for live amphibians,
snappers have that perverse beauty
ugly as memory coming to take you
to the bottom with it. Behind the snap-end
are seven kinds of light to dark meat
that cook up into a stew
fit to satisfy darker appetites.

Cut it bite-size, coat it with pepper-
seasoned flour, stir-fry it in hot oil
enough to seal the chunks. Dump it
and six sliced garlic cloves into a crockpot
set on high. Leave it for two hours.

Peel and slice carrots and potatoes,
dice a big onion and fat bell peppers.
Add this with three bay leaves
and a cup of white wine.
Set pot on low for six more hours.
Stir every two hours.

                    With stirrings
note how aroma deepens toward
the inevitable—Friday supper.
Mix friendship with more wine,
dish up the meal
that's pushed itself up
onto your table by its own four-legged
strokes toward light, out of that
dark part of yourself
you might never have thought
you wanted to face.

    for Hairsn

All the Way

My brother and I'd go east out of town
to hunt, near the Wigand place.
We'd go close
to see the weathered boards
of the two-story house and the barn
and the old man and his machinery
aging in the yard,
then turn south past the cemetery
toward the river.

Old Man Wigand was screwy
and nobody ever saw the old lady.
Charlie was my brother's age,
Pauline a year behind me
in school.
She had deep eyes, dark hair
and skin that made me think
of horsetraders, Moravia,
Gypsies.

The older guys at school said
she'd be nice to anybody
who'd act like
he wanted her to.
I never knew for sure.
After all,
if a guy wanted to go that far
he might as well go all the way
to the river.

Home School

Years before my father taught me to shoot
I watched Mom tie chickens by the legs
on the clothesline a dozen at a time.
With her stropped butcherknife
she'd move quick down the line
slicing beaked and wattled fruit,
never a drop of blood on her.
Neighbors preferred wringing necks,
bodies flopping headless about the yard.
She explained to me, never to them,
how flopping free bruises meat.

She scalded in a bucket, plucked,
gutted in the yard and carried
six-to-a-pan into the house,
birds to be singed over open flame
and scrubbed. Last, fast as a seamstress
could stitch shut a sliced thumb,
she'd clean the dozen hearts,
livers and gizzards. One day
she handed me the knife.

Years have left me to puzzle
how some have come vaguely to think
real pillows and comforters are stuffed
with the gutless stuffing of hollofil,
how gizzards grow in clumps
on styrofoam, and fowl
hatch frozen in plastic sacks.
I've been marked for life,
a warm Sunday-after-dinner feeling
that my mother taught me
sharp knives and small matters,
like giblets.

At Dusk

Calm drift of evening—a pipe,
Wild Turkey, a cured-ash fire:
Through the mist of middle age
an antlered mulie rises,
shakes rut into full bloom.
This is the season of down
pillow and *perina*, of family
coveyed at a round oak
table of game and trimmings.

The first time up the brushy draw
north of town with Dad
and the .410 bolt action
I missed by a canyon-country mile.
Time and a new Model 12
folded rabbits mid-leap, dropped birds—
then years of duckblinds,
strings of dekes like bobbers
waiting out a nibble, over the blocks
orange-footed greenheads hanging.

The season of family—
an old house sold,
a child come
to claim his birthright:
Two mule deer tracks
from an island in the Platte,
a Fulton double twelve-gauge,
two paintings, one a small boy
nursing an ailing pup,
the other mallards, wings set,
orange webbed feet
ready to dip the marsh,
to be hung on a gunroom wall.

for Harry Humes and Don Welch

Maggie

We sit straight on wood chairs
behind gauze curtains in the mortuary Family Room.
On a flowered print dress, soft mauve and white,
her frail hands are thin
as dried and broken sunflower stalks
on asters crushed by fall snow.
Bright three days ago, her closed eyes
exaggerate thin lips that once
laughed clear as the bell on the neck of a retriever.

* * *

Eyes glazed with too many seasons,
the old dog zig-zags in slow motion for scent;
we walk easy, twenty yards apart in a small fallow patch
brittle as crusted eyelids in the last crisp November.

She had once gone into a river of ice
deep enough to top breast waders
after five mallards we'd dropped out of a flock,
the last one a broken-winged hen that almost beat her.
She got it near the far bank when it came up for air,
then fought ice floes one hundred yards back to the blind.
Her eyes, sharp as December light, approved
that mouthful of duck for years of birds.

Now she trembles as birds scatter
seeds and chaff into a whirlwind.
A cock folds in a puff of feathers,
she's on it like a pup at its first quail wing.
Her eyes say it is enough,
the last retrieve a picture on her first.

*   *   *

The preacher is saying she was called
Sis and Mom and Grandma—I guess she was
by some. His words come hollow as dried bones.
How can he know she is always Maggie,
an aunt worthy of having
the best Springer we ever had
named after her?

for Margaret Beck

The Whisper of Bones Grating

Dragging tumors and blindness like loose cargo
enough to founder a freighter on a reef,
from greying muzzle to hindquarters
that can't keep up with the rest of her,
the Springer has passed her good days.
I help her into the pickup cab
she made in one hop last fall.
Then she sat on the seat
watching, anxious for fields and fencerows.
Now she lies on the floor.
I shove a twenty-two in my belt,
put a shovel in the back.

Off the road I lift her out.
She makes the shallow ditch and waits for me
to lift the bottom fence wire.
She heels a straight unsteady line
the half mile of cedar and ash shelterbelt.
The shovel carries heavy as eleven years must
on an old dog pointing the last scent.

I jab the shovel in the ground,
punctuation to whispers of the wind and cedar.
Ash leaves brittle as the season
make a sound like bones grating.

for Barbara and Bob

West of Omaha, By Way of New Caledonia

At Columbus the turn onto 30
brings the nose onto a southwest course
all the way to where the Platte bends back
northwest. The old truck wallows
in the wash of eighteen-wheelers
and a northwest wind.

At Grand Island we side-slip
onto the Standard runway.
The old man at the pump grins:
"Good-soundin' old machine.
I bet she really flies."
The numbers on the pump roll
like a slot machine about to turn up
two plums and a lemon.
The old man talks like an almanac:
"Some wind we're havin'—but you know
what they say about Nebraska weather."
I'm not in the mood: "Yeh. It'll change.
Like in the Gobi Desert." He is:
"Or Siberia." Creases in his weathered face
gave away a sense of humor early.
The credit card machine goes kerchunk.

In the truck I put on sunglasses,
cock my mailorder Australian Sundowner hat,
look at the old man. He grins. I grin
and give him thumbs up like Pappy Boyington
when he's just had his Corsair's wheel chocks
pulled. The engine turns over, I roll
onto the runway, point her between the lines
and give her throttle. I look for the rest
of the squad off and back of my wingtips:
"Let's blow this atoll."

The sun settles into the windscreen
just to right of center. Another few minutes
and it'll settle into the cloudbank that threatens
to snow us under. Eight mission-completed Zeros
race south to home base, like a squadron of crows
scudding across Nebraska sky on a winter wind.

It's February. We're flying
west of Omaha.

———•———

Vagrants

Near the tag-end
of the glory days of the hobo
my brother and I took charge
of garden enough to keep
two boys in weeds a month of summers.
Beans, lettuce, radishes and
an acre and a half of potatoes lined rows
that narrowed in the distance
like railroad tracks. We kept one eye
on the road. Hoboes
would work for a meal.

Stooped, shuffling, hollow-eyed,
pants and shirt flapping in the hot wind
across a clotheshorse body,
he came to the back door.
Dad would say he'd been in jail,
the cops had used a hose on him.
Mom told him he didn't have to work.
"No, ma'am. I can't eat if I ain't worked."

We watched his hands crawl the rows,
knees and toes defining progress
slow as new roads across
unmapped prairie. One bean row
one gust of wind lifted
his shirttail off a lattice-work
of new scars. He more careful than the wind
lifted each hanging plant to
gently pull young foxtail.

Mom would tell him enough,
he would thank her and
shuffle toward the railroad.
Where he left off
we'd scowl up the rows,
enthusiastic as yardbirds
eyeing a lifetime of rockpile.
A steam whistle would signal
drive wheels dragging west
a mile of empty boxcars.

———•———

Blood Brothers

Summer mornings we'd hear the switch engines.
The bump and rattle of coupling cars
hurried our hoes up and down potato rows
so we could go watch real work.
When Mother said good enough
we'd run two blocks to cross
the highway and a hay field
to see Bill ride stockcars
over the hump by the stockyards.
Sitting on top of a railroad car
like a sultan on a magic carpet
he'd turn the big brakewheel
and the car would stop
as if he willed it.
He moonlighted as a butcher.

His old pickup backed
into the maze of wire and boards
Dad had thrown up to raise two pigs.
Bill unloaded his gear, a battered
Winchester .22 pump and a long thin knife.
Mother cautioned us from the porch
to not bother Mr. Schnebly.
"The boys won't be no bother, ma'am."

We stayed near the house as he shot
once, pumped, shot again, each
behind an ear. Gingerly
over garden clods to the back lot
and past two spent cases like eyes
the color of the sun staring in the dust
we walked up to 250 pounds of dead weight
already hung from each side of the rack and
slack across the tailgate. Punctured
arteries streamed into the ground.
"I want to be strong enough to lift
a pig someday." My brother said,
"You'll never be that strong."

Big-eyed at ripples in rounded shoulders
shirtless under overall straps, we watched
rivers of sweat thin the blood of his work.
"A little grisly, ain't it boys?
But it's sure gonna taste good."
Bill winked. Our eyes widened.

He skinned and gutted fast,
cleaned up, picked up, drove off
with the mystery of pig to pork
a dark secret in our minds. After,
when we'd see him on the street and say,
"Hi, Bill," he'd know the ritual.
He'd say, "Hi, boys," and wink.

A muggy summer wrapped our lives
like winding sheets on mummies.
The merciless morning sun, hoe handles,
potato rows and oppressive afternoons
gained on us. Switch engines thumping
cars on the sidetracks
no longer made us look up.

At the end of a row my brother stood
frozen in the pose of a boy studying
a hoe blade half-buried in its next cut.
Shimmering stillness pressed us back
into the dust of the rows. "How come
Dad's comin' home this time of day?"

Mother met him on the porch.
They stood as if for a photograph
neither would want a print of.
She went back into the house.
Dad looked down, then out at us,
waved and was gone up the street's heat wave
like a wraith disappearing into a mirage.
At dinner we tried to digest the news:
Wrong signals had bumped Bill
under tons of tandem wheels,
the artery where his leg had been
could not be held.

At supper Dad said he and Mother
would be going to Schnebly's that evening.
My brother tried to wink at me
over mashed potatoes, pork gravy and roast.

After dishes we went through the garden
to barren ground surrounded by sunflowers
now head-high, boards and posts and rolled wire
neatly stacked. The sun was still hot.

We sat in the dirt, heads down, tears
dark spots on the blood-darkened ground.
My brother cursed the railroad.

—————•—————

A Beautiful
Valley
This

Scot Magic

"You've been drinking." No,
not drinking. I've had a Scotch. Or two.

Mere drinking is what colorless liquid is for.
As an instance, vodka, Mr. Ciardi says,
has no breath at all. And gin? Good God!
The evil it does may be hard to assess, but
anyone of any years who touches the stuff
should be strung up by three fingers, neat.

Scotch, my wife says, smells like gasoline,
low-test, to which I say "You have no taste,
nor smell." Actually, she smells quite good,
sometimes of lilacs before they've gone too far,
sometimes of a fall afternoon that's gone
as good as it can go, which is however here
beside the point. The point is
Scotch is for the tongue tuned to things aged,
like vintage wine you'd bid
a bankroll that's not even yours on.
It's the comfort of a white-haired man
who's been run already hard enough and set
to savor the fire of a winter's night.

Scotch is a constant. At, say, twelve years,
it's never going to be more, nor less,
drinkable. Let's not quibble over blended stuff
some wager in money's stead on sport.
I'm talking about malt, laddie, with names
that sound best on a seasoned Highland tongue.
Cardhu, Knockando, Lagavulin, Laphroaig,
Glendronach, Glenmorangie, The Macallen—Aye,
there're labels you can bet you ex-wife's inheritance
will feel smooth on the tongue as new-conjured gold
distilled in the glen by a kilted alchemist.

A Beautiful Valley This

1

Opening day
an old Fulton, a new Model 12 and we
drove into Potter's yard at dawn.
Seventh-day Adventist, he couldn't shoot
Saturdays. He pointed us into the canyons.
Up that first draw south you doubled pheasant
before I got off my safety.
The fastest I've shot with you showed me
how to shoot true and careful and that
no time remembers better than the first.

2

I was barely big enough to rig a rod and
cars were cheap and didn't bend up much.
Out of bed and daybreak still a piece away
we laughed at your kitchen-craft: pancakes
dark as rusty coffeecan lids on white plates,
a half-dozen eggs frizzled as the parched brim
on an old sun-beat fisherman's hat,
and crisped bacon. We laughed and ate it
all, with real butter and floating in syrup,
back when cholesterol and carcinoma weren't yet
blips on the radar of public conscience.

West of town a half-mile a car dived
off the bridge like a merganser at a minnow.
"That bird went to sleep at the wheel," you said.
That bird and the summer pre-dawn
half-light detoured all our trips
into the creek. He and his car
weren't bad hurt, and I learned
you have to be flexible
as an eight-foot spinning rod and fish
don't much seem to notice
what time of day an early bird dangles
a fresh-dug garden worm in their lake.

3

Our blind on the island
was eight feet above water, a box
hid by early-cut willow and plum.
Six mergansers kamikazied us headon,
their error giving us dawn at our backs.
We knocked three in the river, a fourth
blammed the board-fence front thigh-high,
the survivors thrumming past our hats
like prehistoric hummingbirds. Nice warmup
for us and the dog, you said, counting on
mallards the rest of the day.

4

You started it.
"A beautiful valley
this Elkhorn River Valley."
We were headed for McCoy Cemetery
where your dad and brother are buried.
You don't know their middle names.
"Grandad Crook came here
one hundred fourteen years ago,
bought land for fifty cents an acre."

We drove past concrete slabs of progress
lying like alkali beds around shopping malls
and argued signs, signs of prosperity
you called them.
West of here good farm ground
goes for near four hundred
with no takers. Keya Paha pasture
might bring thirty-five,
dry years and grass fires
thrown in no charge.

Coming back the old road
you said that row of cottonwoods
was already big when you were a boy.
They reminded you to say you'd had enough
woodcutting, gangsaw and ax,
didn't think you wanted to live
that life over. That afternoon you eyed
my chainsaw like the moneyed half
an interest in a business
you were interested in once—maybe
you could ease back into it.
Then you said, "Looks like work,
I'm glad it's yours."

5

Three winters' fires
fill the ash pit to seven feet,
enough to treat the retired
neighbor's garden for more years
than he'll ever need. The chill
hanging in the air this evening says
the pit has to be cleaned. Elm and ash
split and cured are corded
behind the garage.
As if from a movie projector
running on the juice of your lifetime,
the flickering light and playful
shadows of the first fall fire
keep us all quiet as smoke.

for John E. Holland, 1905 or 1906 to 1992

It's Not Right to Expect
Something for Nothing

The daily news is fuzzy
but my eye's still sharp enough
to spot a leaf's turn into fall.
Telephone talk and the neighbor's chatter
fade like a weak radio beam,
but my ear still picks up a squirrel's chirr.
My legs have lost the drive
that once shed linebackers like alders
snapped in a bull elk's wake
and mountains keep getting higher.
A bifocal assist will clear up bad news,
I can get battery-op trumpets to hear
enough of the neighbor, and football
has to be passé. I'm still
quick enough to feel the heart tighten,
blood burn at the height.
If the equipment gets me where
thin air is clear and carries
the elk's shrill and the marmot's bark
and I see, by the gods, for ever,
there's no more to wish for.

Wrong Foot Forward

To fall off a mountain be right choosy
about boot placement, planting one carefully
on granite, the other deftly heel-first
on rain-soaked lichen. Feel the sponge
slip, know all the way to your socks
you're airborne. The instant
your butt flattens the boulder see
your hat like a doughnut on edge race
you toward treeline. Bounce like a bad hop
on a hard infield and stop cold against a pine
bole rough as the last mountainman.
In the shroud that echoes silence, lie back,
look straight up the trunk to branches gathered
harmless as a Christmas tree against a slate sky.
Eye your scraped palm, know your wrist will swell
and offer small thanks to whatever gods
guard flatlanders in hiking shoes that
the pain in your ribs isn't
poking out through your shirt. Stand,
still, 'til your quivering thighs
tell your knees it's ok to bend. Find
your hat, recrease it, put it on—
tight. Ease down the slope, hunker
by the fire. Grind your teeth, softly,
as your partner passes
the 100-proof painkiller and says
"I damnear fell on my ass up there."

The Length of Shadows

I imagined him
standing under the depot roof,
lifting it from the right vest pocket
by its burnished gold chain,
pushing the stem with his thumb
to snap open the case,
other thumb hooked in the left.
He would look down the tracks,
then down again to his hand.
He'd say, "On time."

I got it as a tarnished case,
hinged, with a worn clasp.
No hands pointed out
Roman numerals on the white face.
I don't carry it
with any need to track time
beyond lengthening shadows,
the feel of a day.
I carry it because
my father handed it to me
after the funeral:
"This was your mother's father's.
Thought you might want it."

No time left for a wife
and two daughters, he died
when she was four.
Mom went to eighty-six,
not knowing entirely
what time of day
or whose lifetime it was.

Shiny as a rubbed doubloon,
wound every morning and admired
several times a day at arm's length,
its mainspring coils
a third generation.
The jeweler said this one
was never railroad perfect
and never would be.
I hold it in my hand,
in my own sweet time.

for JV Brummels and Jack Putters

———•———

OTHER POEMS

This Is My Body

The choir loft of First Church,
at the front of the sanctuary one step
above the congregation and beyond the communion rail,
its three rows of straight-backed chairs set
like dominoes waiting for a push, offered the choir
up each Sunday as the only show in town.

I, my key in the piano of life stuck
in the uncertain miracle of adolescent bass,
languished there like Herakles trying to avoid labors
no worse than pimples and terminal thoughts of erections
initiated by glimpses of devout sopranos.
Only during communion, once a quarter, when
the congregation would file Catholic-style
to the altar to kneel before flat grape juice
and flatter crackers, could anyone else
have the pleasure of being seen by everyone.
It was occasion to be dressed right.

From near the back, from under the stained-glass
Son-of-God south window, Ben came
expectant as a bride shopping for a wedding dress
all the way to the rail. Shaved, scrubbed,
decked out, a Druid marching to sacrifice, left hand
hanging loose by the impeccable dark-grey trouser leg,
right thumb jutting straight ahead, those missing fingers
lost to a jump-saw years before in his last bout
with physical effort, Ben was set to win
the dress parade. The woman in front of him
turned down the rail. Ben stepped up.

His jacket's reaction to his kneeling
exposed his unzipped fly.
Like a bleached and starched thumb,
a shirttail pointed out the choir.
Pious as a preacher demonstrating piety
to a confirmation class, he prayed.
He drank. He chewed. He arose.
The white projection caught in his jacket front,
Ben rode smiling and oblivious the straight and narrow
crest of tittered Methodist restraint to his pew,
assurance of the resurrection still in his mouth.

———◦———

Walk On Water

I knew a man once
who could witch water:
hazel stick in hand
he'd walk
like a man on thin ice
until the stick would quiver
and he'd sink a well and hit water
and that would be that.
I always imagined I could do that.
One day I cut a hazel stick
and walked,
but didn't feel
like a man on thin ice,
the hazel stick stuck straight out in front of me,
and nobody came to ask me where to dig.

for Paul and Jim

Eleven Days

The sun sets
a blood-shot stare
through the bones
of western treelines
where the chain-link fence runs out.
The snowdrift, monument to December's record
chill that crystallized the back yard
in its tracks, is no longer high
and hard and white and marble
untouched.

Eleven days ago, the day
a bright and balmy end
to a month of sundogs,
the rabbit from under the deck
came to the edge of the fence
to sniff the remains
of refrigerator-defrosting.
Later, a ball of fluff
still in the sun,
she warmed with the days
that thawed lettuce and carrots
limp pastels into the snow.

Eight days ago, slit-eyed,
tail-drooping and twitching,
a fat yellow cat lolled
on the deck rail, like sun-
rise to a clear day.

Stark links of fence
mark a low sound.
Yesterday's snow remains
untracked.

The Window

Next door to my father's
they're building a garage,
two men with stomachs hanging
over belts, jeans without hammer loops
pulling down behind when they bend
to nail plates to studs
for walls. My father and I watch
through the pantry window
where my mother stood watching
years of weather and him
come home from building
houses, garages, cabinets, once
two quonset huts for hay storage,
always from the plans up.
His stomach never hung
over his nail apron.

If he could reach behind
to tie a nail apron, his stomach
would not hang over it.
Though he strains to tie his shoes,
if he could bend to the studs
laid out like a cell door
and hold a hammer,
his arthritic left hand
would drive nails straight.
I know this as he says
how the walls will tie together
this new garage, how two-by-twelve headers
will span the opening for overhead doors,
his eyes still reading blueprints.

———◆———

Try to Remember

Fragile as grandmother's leaded heirloom crystal,
she waits at the table
in the corner facing the parquet floor,
furtive glance ready
for a sign from a dance-floor Adonis.
Patience that enhances the dark underside
of her hourglass figure
in the chance
of certain attraction.

Subtly schooled,
she to remember the family name
and act her age,
he his gamesmanship
and good manners
that neutralize the fear
that he will ask before
her web has tangled him,
like two fingers caught in frenetic hair
they will bob and weave the last dance.

Predictable as winter's fulfillment
she sits in her corner
alone, weaving,
memory by memory.

How to Acquire a Beard

In an almost post-seedy state
a faceful of bristles prompts
at least careful repartee.
The insurance man in his three-piece
and button-down with repp striped tie
asks, "Doesn't it itch?" I say,
"No. I never keep anything
I have to scratch." The wife
says, "I like you better with just
your moustache" and later "Why don't you
shave some from your cheekbones?"
Mother says, "You look like Hemingway."
My deep-browed brother says, "His shape
is wrong. It's just another white beard."
The aging worriers say, in chorus, "You could
use shoe polish." What begins as escape from
Marine-like daily discipline after months of days
comes to full fluff; the sweet thing across the hall
says, "I just love your beard," and flaps her lashes
and wiggles. When the wife scowls and asks,
"Isn't it time to trim it?"
you know you've hit the big time.

——•——

Mutability

I heard today
Murray died,
just slumped over
in his pasture.
Small matter,
near as I could tell;
nobody cared,
at least nobody I know.

Oh around town
I'd see him odd-man
for coffee every morning
around the big table at the café,
and he paid his bills on time
as cattlemen do.

But he had his seamy side
the old biddies would squint
their eyes over—story was
he had something going
with the waitress
and his wife was tired
and divorced him.
I wondered why he never seemed
to run around after that.

Predictable as Spring
he never allowed
the pristine vaulted church
to darken his brow.
Predictable as Fall
his children and grandchildren
will come to the funeral.

Friday Night

Dew on the backyard grass
soaks my shoes on the weekly trip
to and from the trashcan.
The forecast of rain is a hollow threat
forgotten in rafted clouds thinner than the Milky Way.

The moon, one night past full,
dodges the leaves in Lou's Buckeye.
You call from Jack's to ask
what else is on the list you didn't take.
When you get back we'll dream
Friday night dreams on the deck
and drink ourselves lucky on Tanqueray.

for Beck

Of Patriarchs, Dowagers, Cats and Zucchini

THE ALLEY

My first day in the alley
he hobbled up on his stick.
"I'm Vic. Live in the two-story
grey, over there." His stick
jabbed northeast, wielded like a sceptre
but quirt-quick, so it could get back
under him. He'd been out of the hospital
three weeks, broken hip. "Doc says
I should walk. I can't get
run over in the alley."

"Good neighborhood. Lou there
has eleven goddamn cats, though."
This time his sceptre jabbed due east.
"And Maita here next to you,
she's lived alone all these years—
be eighty-nine in October."

Maita had been in the house
since 1928. "Never married," she said.
"My sister did that. I came to take care of
my father. He died thirty-five years ago."
She'd taught one-room schools in Brown County
before becoming her father's keeper.

Vic was going on. "Over there's
Jim and his wife. Retired from the railroad.
Do anything for you. Goddamn nosy, too, talk yer arm off.
Keeps this big goddamn garden in Maita's yard.
Keeps him from drivin' his wife crazy.
Only racket here comes from the blue house.
Next to mine. Junior high boys."
I had boxes to sort.
Vic gimped down the alley.

Lou

Lou hollered over did we want some tomatoes.
We did. I said I hadn't seen much of Vic this summer.
"Oh that goddamn Vic! In the hospital again.
Tripped over his hose, broke five ribs
on the sidewalk." Didn't he break his hip
last year? "Oh yes. Had his house shingled.
Up there checking did they do it right.
Fell off his goddamn roof."

Jim

I was out back watching two police
officers trying to collar cats
in the storm sewers on Lou's corner.
Jim stopped, his pickup mounded with melons.
"Goddamn cats. Mess up the yard,
dig in the garden. Got me a pellet gun.
Sure makes 'em run." Later, Jim would tell me
the cops took seven to the pound.

I asked where his melon patch was.
"Don't have one. Helpin' an old geezer
too feeble to tend his. Gives me
a pickup load every year. Zucchini too.
I pass 'em around. Your wife make zucchini bread?"
I lied, said she does.

"Seen Vic's cast?" I hadn't.
"Broke his arm. Propped his stick against the door,
fell off his back step." I allowed
he must be pretty old and brittle.
"That goddamn Vic's eighty-six,
gonna outlive us all. Lives alone,
takes care of the house, mows the yard.
Still drives to town every day."
I wondered what for. Jim said,
"Practicin' bein' stubborn."
Jim left us four zucchini, big ones.

THE BLUE-HOUSE BOYS

Spring. Blue-house boys and friends were running
like buffalo calves through tall prairie
their daily dinner-hour game of
block-sized hide and seek. Jim, Vic and I
were in our yards and fed up.
"You! Come over here!" Vic had one
in his sights. "One of you boys
mashed some of my flowers."
The boy said he hadn't.
Vic's sceptre jabbed the ground,

like underscore and exclamation marks.
"Yeh, I know, it wasn't *you*.
Never *is*. But I'm talkin' to *you*!
And I'm tellin' *you* it better *stop*!
Now, goddamnit!"

Next night, so quiet you could hear
sprouts pushing out of the ground,
I heard Vic. His voice ricocheted
off the blue house and around the block
like a ball off a new-strung racquet.
"Jim, c'mon over!" I could see him
waving his sceptre like Crazy Horse
ready to count coup. "We're gonna
have some fun! Nobody mashes
my goddamn flowers again
without *me* around their necks!"

MAITA

I'd taken her a first-try zucchini bread loaf.
"A peaceful neighborhood, Maita." She agreed,
added how kind folks are. Lou checks on her,
Jim brings garden things,
an older boy on the block mows her lawn.

A cat came down the sidewalk, stopped and stared.
She picked up the broom. The cat, as if
a light bulb over its head had blinked on,
padded back into the alley. A long blast
on the horn of a faded green sedan
sent it in cat leaps for Lou's. Vic's Rambler
swirled dust devils up the alley to his garage.

Maita waved her broom toward the Rambler.
I raised a hand palm out and thought
how Vic is in charge of the alley,
the entire neighborhood. And how
I'm goddamn glad he is.

for Vic Schleuter, in memoriam

An Act of God

We stop to photograph
the old church in the pasture,
the mist dulled-grey
water beads that hung like dust
on unbrowsed bluestem and spring cedar,
the chill a pleasant walk in the dooryard
beneath a Rose window of random broken stained-
glass like abandoned farm windows shot
by city Vandals. Inside
the sanctuary balcony supports
a basketball goal, worn net hanging
like a cobweb.

"God's workout room," you say.
The b-ball goal hung from the balcony with care
in hopes God would bless us in our underwear.
Your odd look agrees with my thought:
"Bless us, Father, for we are about to sin."

I rush to the car for the emergency blanket—
this is emergency zealots burn for.
Later, straight above
a sparrow nest decorates a chandelier,
its one bulb the eye of a hurricane half-passed,
hanging by three rusted chains; on single chains
two more droop like spilled Easter baskets.

"Isn't that odd," you giggle,
"how hard this floor is. There's a pile
of hay in the school. Must be used
only by Catholics." I, always willing to learn,
ask why. "Because there are no rubbers
anywhere there." True, but some unenlightened
Protestants have been known to live dangerously, too.
Quick as a vicar at newly discovered sin, you say,
"No Protestant would screw in a church,
at least not with his eyes open."

In the wreckage of the bathroom
under the bird-crusted stairs, I put the lid down
and go upstairs and out. The cedars
your aura, the corners of your mouth rise
only slightly. Ever fond of testing
post-Methodist sensibility, you ask,
"Did you put the lid down?"
I hang my head as affirmation.
"How come you never do at home?"
At home I am God.
"You might be here too."
The dark flash of your eyes a Genesis,
I think, by God, I might be.

Afterword

In the summer of 1981 I took a creative writing class at what was then Northeast Technical Community College. The instructor was a man in his forties whose ready smile told me that here was someone who was excited and amused by life and who really enjoyed what he was doing with it. His name, he told us, was Larry Holland, and his positive attitude toward life and toward writing about life was contagious.

A week or so later our new instructor was absent and Barbara Schmitz took over the class, explaining that Larry had shattered his shoulder in a softball game. Barbara taught the class for several weeks while Larry underwent surgery and physical therapy for an injury that he confided in me later had him wondering if he might lose his left arm.

When he returned, other than carrying his arm in a sling and a good deal of metal in his left shoulder, Larry seemed like the same smiling person he had been a few weeks earlier. And as far as his students knew he was the same instructor, excited about life and writing. I doubt whether any of his students or many of his friends knew the depth of his psychological pain in dealing with his injury, or the effort he put into overcoming the physical limitations that resulted from it. I knew Larry's physical therapist, and she related something of his therapy, how hard he worked to save his arm and regain as much use of it as he could.

Some months afterward, Larry told me his left arm had shrunk to half its original size. And though his intense efforts at therapy gave him back much, he never did regain the full use of his left arm. He gave up bowhunting with his sixty-five-pound Bear recurve because he could no longer lock the shoulder of his bow arm against the pull of his right at full draw. After his injury we did a lot of backpacking, canoeing, and later horsebacking together, and I often sensed his frustration with the limited use of his arm and the pain he underwent to continue doing the things he loved to do in spite of his handicap. Still, he never gave any outward sign of his internal struggles.

So it should have come as no surprise to me to learn I'd been canoeing and backpacking for a number of years with a man who had a serious heart condition. I found out after our final climb up the Palmer Lake trail, shortly before Larry had surgery to repair leaking valves he'd been carrying since a childhood bout with rheumatic fever.

Larry always got sick on our climbs into the Bridger Wilderness area of the Wind River Mountains, and he always claimed it was just mountain sickness caused by the altitude change. But going up those godless switchbacks on the Palmer Lake trail that last time I think we both knew there was a bit more to it than that. I've wondered since if Larry knew exactly what the problem was, maybe had known for years, and just decided to let nature take whatever course she chose each time we went on one of our excursions into the mountains. I know we both commented often enough that you couldn't find a better place to die than the Wind River Mountains. God knows just how close Larry came to it the last time we went up the Palmer Lake trail.

For someone as oriented toward life in the outdoors as Larry Holland, such incidents as shattering his shoulder or discovering his weakened heart had to have a tremendous impact. So it is significant to me that Larry never wrote directly about either occurrence, or about the effects each had on the course of his life. But I want to emphasize the word "directly" here, because I believe the reader who is aware of these two incidents in Larry's life may well find evidence of their effects in a number of the poems he wrote.

Look again at "It's Not Right to Expect Something for Nothing." Larry Holland knew through personal experience that life included a good deal of pain and a certain degree of frustration with the aging process. Both serve as necessary reminders that as long as we live we are also engaged in the process of dying. If we can learn to accept such experiences as unavoidable and necessary, and not waste our lives regretting what we cannot change, I believe, as Larry did, that we can still get to "where thin air is clear and...there's no more to wish for."

—Neil Harrison
Norfolk, Nebraska
July 2001